BE KIND TO YOUR DOG AT CHRISTMAS *and Other Ways to Have*

Happy Holidays and a Lucky New Year

by Barbara Heine Costikyan

Pictures by Joyce Audy dos Santos

PANTHEON BOOKS · NEW YORK

For Nancy, José and Ana Cedillo, on their first Christmas together
B. H. C.

For my friend Ana Sanchez and her lovely family
J. A. D. S.

"Leave a loaf" (page 13), "Green branch" (page 26), "Eat an apple" (page 18), "Two kinds of holly" (page 27) are adapted from pp. 105, 45, 105, 51 in *All About Christmas* by Maymie R. Krythe. Copyright 1954 by Maymie Richardson Krythe. Reprinted by permission of Harper & Row, Publishers, Inc.

"White horse" (page 43), "Keep the mistletoe" (page 28) are adapted from pp. 504, 732 in *Funk & Wagnalls Standard Dictionary of Folklore, Mythology and Legend*, edited by Maria Leach. Copyright 1949, © 1950, 1972 by Harper & Row, Publishers, Inc. Reprinted by permission of Harper & Row, Publishers, Inc.

"Sleepy hen" (page 31) is adapted from p. 76 of *Christmas the World Over*, by Daniel J. Foley. Copyright 1963 by the author. Reprinted with the permission of the publisher, Chilton Book Company, Radnor, PA.

FIRST EDITION

Library of Congress Cataloging in Publication Data. Costikyan, Barbara. Be kind to your dog at Christmas. Summary: A collection of Christmas superstitions from around the world, including ways to achieve a year of good luck and protect your pets. 1. Superstition—Juvenile literature. 2. Christmas—Juvenile literature. [1. Superstition. 2. Christmas] I. Dos Santos, Joyce "Audy," ill.   I. Title BF1775.C62   1982   394.2'68282   81-22343
ISBN 0-394-84963-9   ISBN 0-394-94963-3 (lib. bdg.)   AACR2

# Contents

 # Introduction

Onions, shoes, apples, bread, pots, broomsticks—even a front door may have special powers at Christmas and can bring good luck in the year ahead. But you have to know what to do and what not to do with everyday objects like these to make them lucky. In this book you'll find things to do for a merry Christmas season and a lucky New Year, based on customs and beliefs from many parts of the world.

For many centuries, people have believed that what happens around the new year can actually decide the future. This belief goes back to an important festival celebrated long ago, before there was a holiday called Christmas or a month named December. It was a festival of fire that welcomed the new year and honored the sun. It was held in midwinter when the days were dark, yet people knew that soon the sun should begin its slow journey to the top of the sky; the days would lengthen, and spring would come. Every year, they wanted to make sure this would happen again, so to help the sun on its voyage and to remind it to shine brightly they burned candles and built great fires from trees, often trees that were cut down at sunrise. They believed that these fires, which gave light and warmth in the dead of winter, had life-giving powers just like the sun's. The ashes were thought to cure sickness, and bread or meat cooked over the flames was supposed to give strength to whoever ate some.

To people long ago, deep winter was a time of rest. With the crops harvested, there was little work to do, so they feasted on the fruits of the harvest, they sang and danced, wore silly costumes, played noisy games, shared sweet-tasting foods to insure peace in the year ahead, and sat around the fire. But in the midst of the merrymaking, they feared that evil spirits walked the dark night outside; to scare them away, bells were clanged and pots were banged. And they watched the sky, the wind, their animals for signs that good luck would come to their families and their farms.

As centuries passed, Christmas replaced these festivals, but the old ideas and rites stayed on. People went on burning logs at Christmas and baking Christmas bread. And ordinary objects were still thought to bring luck during the twelve days between Christmas Eve and Twelfth Night (January 6). On this last day of Christmas, in many countries, the ox in the barn and an old apple tree are still part of a joyous celebration to bring about a lucky crop.

Today, you don't have to own an ox or an apple tree to try for good luck at Christmastime—you can use your own front door or a loaf of bread. Our Christmases are bright with electric lights, and we aren't afraid of a dark cold night. But all the same, we feel the power of Christmas and know how important everyday things still can be—just as they were long ago.

THE TWELVE DAYS OF CHRISTMAS

If you want to have one whole year of good luck, eat a mince pie every day during the Twelve Days of Christmas. Each pie must be baked by a different cook. Each pie must be eaten in a different place. One pie equals one month's good luck. Twelve pies make a lucky year.

CHRISTMAS EVE

Bang pots and pans in front of your house on Christmas Eve. Do this as loudly as you can. The noise will scare away bad luck.

You should also stick a loaf of bread on a broomstick and leave it out in front of your house overnight. Bad luck won't come your way all year.

A big log that gives a bright Christmas fire is called the Yule log. For an especially lucky Yule log, cut down an oak tree a few days before Christmas. Be sure it falls to the east at the exact moment the sun comes up. Don't take it indoors until after sunset on Christmas Eve. The oldest and youngest person in the house should each carry one end of the log.

Sneeze at the dinner table on Christmas Eve and you'll have a good night's sleep.

When you have finished Christmas Eve dinner, leave a loaf of bread on the table overnight. If you do this, your family will have plenty of bread in the year to come.

Blow out a candle, then open the window as fast as you can. If the smoke goes straight up in the air, it's a lucky sign. If the smoke goes out the window, it's a sign of bad luck.

Put some animal food in your pocket before you go to church on Christmas Eve. Afterwards, feed it to your pets, and they'll be healthy all year.

If the moon shines into the stable after church on Christmas Eve, the harvest will be bad. If the stable is dark after church, the harvest will be good.

Dig up twelve onions on Christmas Eve night. The onions should all be the same size. Name each onion for a different month of the year. Put salt on the onions, then put them in a dark place. Don't look at them until Twelfth Night. The onions that are wet on Twelfth Night will stand for next year's rainy months. The dry onions will be months without rain.

Dig up four more onions. Name each onion after a different sweetheart. Put one onion in each corner of your room. The sweetheart whose name is on the first onion to grow a shoot will be your true love.

Bake Christmas bread by the light of the moon on Christmas Eve, *never* when the sun's up. If the dough rises especially high, you're going to have a lucky year.

If the sky is full of stars on Christmas Eve, there'll be a big crop of peas in June.

If you play this old-fashioned game on Christmas Eve, your Christmas wish may come true:

Everybody sits around the table. At each place there's a tiny unlighted candle, like a birthday candle. One person starts the game by lighting a candle and telling a little story that includes a Christmas wish. If the story is finished at the same time the candle goes out, the wish will come true.

The next person also tells a story with a wish in it, trying to finish at the same moment the candle burns out. Everybody at the table takes a turn. But when the clock strikes midnight, the game has to stop because it's Christmas Day.

Here are three things to do at midnight on Christmas Eve:

Open your front door and let in the good luck. Open the back door and let out the bad luck.

Tie a rope around a fruit tree to remind it to bear fruit in the spring.

Eat an apple on the stroke of midnight and you won't catch a cold all year.

Mix a cake before you go to bed on Christmas Eve. From the moment you begin, be sure not to say a word to anyone. With a fork or toothpick, prick your own initials on the cake. Put the cake in the warm ashes of the fireplace to bake and go to bed, without saying anything. If you find any other initials on the cake in the morning, they will be the initials of the person you'll marry. (This cake is *not* meant to be eaten!)

To guard the Christmas pies from bad luck, put them under your bed when you go to sleep.

If all the members of your family put their shoes in a row before going to bed on Christmas Eve, there won't be any fighting in the year ahead.

Each person in the house should write the names of two people on slips of paper. Put the slips into a big bowl. In the morning, pull out two of the slips. The two people whose names are on these slips will either be good friends or marry each other in the new year.

If your dog howls on Christmas Eve, it's a sign he'll go crazy in the new year, so be kind to your dog at Christmas.

CHRISTMAS DAY

The first person who wakes up on Christmas Day should open the front door and shout, "Welcome, Father Christmas!" This brings good luck to the whole house.

This person should also take a broom and sweep all the bad luck out of the house.

Feed your pets by candlelight on Christmas Day, before the sun rises, and they will behave well all year long.

If you eat a raw egg on Christmas morning, you'll be strong all year.

It's bad luck to wear new leather shoes on Christmas morning.

On Christmas morning, get on a swing and swing as high as you can. This will remind the sun to climb to the top of the sky in summer.

Ring bells loudly on Christmas Day to scare away bad luck.

If the sun shines through the church windows on Christmas morning, it will be a good year for fruit.

The day of the week when Christmas falls can help you predict next year's weather:

MONDAY   A very cold winter and a very rainy summer.
TUESDAY   A rainy year.
WEDNESDAY   A fine summer.
THURSDAY   A bad year for the farm, so sell everything!
FRIDAY   Dry weather.
SATURDAY   Bad weather all year.
SUNDAY   "If Christmas on a Sunday be, A windy winter we shall see."

To find out how much freezing weather there will be next May, count the hours of sunshine on Christmas. An old rhyme says:

> Hours of sun on Christmas Day—
> So many frosts in the month of May.

A windy Christmas is a sign of good luck.

If you get a sunburn on your nose at Christmas, you will burn your toe at Easter.

If you have a heart-shaped box, fill it with candy at Christmas, because an empty heart will bring bad luck in the year to come.

Don't haul anything in a wagon or use an eggbeater on Christmas Day, because it's bad luck to do any work where wheels are supposed to turn.

Don't give away anything from the house on Christmas Day—money, food, wood, or even garbage—unless somebody brings something into the house *first*. Otherwise, good luck will go out with the gift.

It's especially unlucky to give away fire at Christmas. No one should offer anyone a light or even give away a match on Christmas Day.

Never wash a Christmas present before you give it to somebody, or you'll wash away the good luck.

Go hug an apple tree on Christmas Day so it will wake up and bear fruit in the spring.

You'll have good luck if you touch somebody with a green branch on Christmas.

To avoid bad luck, you should have both holly and mistletoe in the house at Christmas. There should be two kinds of holly, prickly and smooth. If the prickly kind is brought into the house first, the husband will run the house in the new year; if the smooth kind is brought in first, the wife will rule. But if both come in at the same time, husband and wife will agree.

Take six holly leaves. Wrap them in a handkerchief and put them under your pillow. You'll dream of the person you will marry.

It's bad luck to step on a holly berry.

Put a tiny candle on a holly leaf and light the candle. Put the leaf in water. If it floats, you will have good luck.

Keep holly berries all year for good luck. For more good luck, keep the Christmas mistletoe, too, and burn it under next year's Christmas pudding.

To share Christmas luck with your animals, put holly where they can see it on Christmas Day.

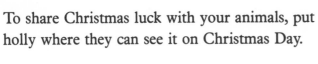

Put some holly on the beehive. If you're kind to the bees, you'll hear them hum carols.

Give your cow a Christmas present and she will give you plenty of milk all year.

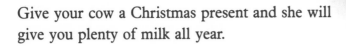

Take your horse to a brook and ride him upstream. Throw an apple into the brook. If it hits the horse, he will grow strong.

If you wash your horse with a fine cloth on Christmas morning, he'll be healthy in the new year.

To tell the future on Christmas Day, put five piles of seed on the floor. One pile stands for love. One pile stands for a long trip. One pile stands for sickness. One pile stands for riches. One pile stands for hard work. Go find a sleepy hen and get her to walk into the room. The first pile the hen pecks at will tell you what's going to happen to you in the new year.

A cricket chirping on Christmas Day is a lucky sign.

If you want to say something about a rat or a mouse on Christmas Day, never say "that rat" or "that mouse," which would make them feel more important and be much pestier. Call a mouse "that little one," call a rat "that big one," and they won't make trouble in the new year.

It's bad luck to go fishing on Christmas Day.

When you visit somebody's house on Christmas Day, be sure to eat the food they offer you. If you refuse to eat in their house, you will take their Christmas spirit away when you leave.

When Christmas dinner is done, take the tablecloth outside and shake the crumbs onto the ground. A plant will grow where the crumbs have fallen. This plant will cure sickness.

If you bury the bones from the Christmas roast under a fruit tree, the tree will bear lots of fruit in the year ahead.

Christmas cake brushed with Christmas morning dew is lucky cake.

A sailor should take a piece of Christmas cake to sea. If he throws it on the water in a big storm, that storm will stop and the sea will calm down.

Save the crumbs from your Christmas cake and keep them until they are dry. When you have a cold, mix the dry crumbs with water and drink the mixture. You'll get better soon.

Mix Christmas cake crumbs with food for your animals and they will be strong all year.

Keep Christmas cake until it's time to plant seeds in your garden. Mix some cake with the seed. Your garden will flourish.

Hit a log in the fire on Christmas Day with the poker. Count the sparks that fly. Each spark stands for a chicken that will be hatched in your chicken coop in the coming year.

Take an old shoe or a handful of salt and throw it into the fire. If there's a loud noise or an awful smell, it will keep bad luck away from your house.

If you visit a house where there's a big Yule log burning, tip your hat to the log. This sign of respect will bring you good luck.

Leave your Yule log in the fireplace till Twelfth Night. Then keep the remains to light next year's log. You'll have a lucky year.

When the charcoal from the Yule log is completely cold, put a piece under your bed. This will protect your house from fire.

Bury ashes from the Yule log in your garden and you'll have a fine crop.

If you hurt yourself, take a piece of charcoal from the Yule log and draw a circle exactly where it hurts. The bump or sore will go away.

If your family is apart on Christmas, each of you should light a candle at the same time and think of the others.

NEW YEAR'S EVE

If you wear something new on New Year's Eve, you will have beautiful clothes all year long.

If you walk into a house with mud on your shoes New Year's Eve, you'll bring luck into the house.

If the wind blows from the south on New Year's Eve, it means a good year for crops.

If it blows from the east, the fruit trees will bear well.

If it blows from the north or the northeast, it means a year with lots of storms.

Put a piece of bread outside the house on New Year's Eve. Take it indoors the next morning. This will bring health, wealth, and happiness to your family in the new year.

On New Year's Eve, take two wooden sticks. Name one stick after a girl and the other after a boy. Put them into the fire. If the sticks burn and curl toward each other, the boy and girl love each other truly. If the sticks burn quickly, they will have a life of happiness. If the sticks curl away from each other, the boy and girl aren't meant for each other.

It's good luck to dream about an eggplant on New Year's Eve.

NEW YEAR'S DAY

If the first thing you say on New Year's Day is "White rabbit, black hares," you'll get a present by the end of January.

Make a wish on the first white horse you see, and your wish will come true.

On New Year's Day, open the front door, take a
broom, and sweep in all the good luck.

For good luck, the first person to enter your house
in the New Year should be a tall man with lots of
dark hair. He should be carrying wood, money, and
a piece of bread, and he should step in with his
right foot first. If a short man with red hair is the
first to come in, it's bad luck.

It's good luck to eat grapes on New Year's Day.

It's also good luck to eat cabbage or spinach. (A green vegetable stands for lots of money in the year to come.)

Don't give anything away or throw anything away on New Year's Day, or good luck will leave with it.

Never wash clothes on that day, or you will wash away all the good luck.

Seven is a lucky number for the new year. Ask seven friends to your house. Serve them seven cakes, seven fruits, seven kinds of ice cream, and seven glasses of water taken from seven fountains. You'll all have good luck.

TWELFTH NIGHT

On Twelfth Night, drink a toast to your cow with apple cider. She will be healthy all year and will give plenty of milk.

For dessert on Twelfth Night, you should have a special cake with beautiful icing and flowers made of sugar on top and a big dried bean baked inside. Cut the cake into as many slices as there are people to be served, and choose a small child to sit under the table. As each slice is put onto a plate, ask the child under the table who should be given that piece of cake. When everyone else has been served, the child can come out from under the table and have some cake. The person who gets the slice with the bean becomes King or Queen of the Bean and will have a year of good luck.

You should have another special cake for Twelfth Night, a plum cake with a large hole in the middle. Take this cake to the barn and put it on an ox's horn. If the ox doesn't toss his head, tickle him with a feather or throw some apple cider on him. (If he tosses his head without being tickled, it's a sign of extra good luck for the farm.) If the cake falls behind the ox, it means a poor harvest. But if it falls in front of him, the harvest will be good.

After supper on Twelfth Night, go outdoors with your family and all your friends. Visit the oldest apple tree. Shout, whistle, bang a spoon on the tree trunk. Pour cider onto the roots. Put a piece of toast soaked in cider onto the branches. This will make the tree wake up from its winter sleep and remember to give apples in the spring.

Say this poem to the apple tree:

> Here's to thee, old apple tree!
> Stand fast, root; bear well, top!
> Pray God send us a good howling crop.
> Every little bough,
> Bear an apple now.
> Every little twig,
> Bear an apple big—
> Hats full, caps full,
> Three quarter-sacks full,
> And a little heap under the stairs!

This drives away bad spirits from the trees and makes the apples grow well.

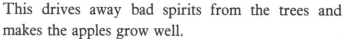

Acknowledgments

The material in this book has been adapted from folklore, primarily European and North American. Letters from folklore scholars reported many ongoing traditions; other material was gathered from printed sources. Where possible, the country or area where each custom has been reported in the form given here has been indicated, yet many traditions exist in many places, all in different forms.

The author gratefully acknowledges the cordial responses of Dr. Jacqueline Simpson, The Folklore Society, London, and Roy Vickery, The London Folklore Group. Gratitude is also expressed to Holger Janssen, Seminar für Volkskunde der Universität Kiel, Germany; to Claude Mauron, Université de Provence (Aix-Marseille), France; to Cecil R. Humphery-Smith, Institute of Heraldic and Genealogical Studies, Canterbury, England; to Joseph Aregger, Vice-Consul General, Switzerland, for his help; and to Meryle Evans and Susan Samuelson for their research.

Special thanks also to Kitty Costikyan, Constance Bickford, Tatiana Davidson, Ulla Jorgensen, and Harry Hunsbedt for Christmas legends they remembered from childhood; to Sylvia Colodner for her encouragement always; to Colette and Marianne Rossant for their translations of French folklore; to Diane De Voe and Sally Bickford for preparing the mailing of questionnaires to folklorists; and to my husband, Edward N. Costikyan, whose idea it was—unknowingly—for me to write this book: his offer to change my Christmas birthday to any day I wished prompted me to discover how very special Christmas is.

B. H. C.

Notes

p. 11. *Mince pie*: England. Courtesy Cecil R. Humphery-Smith, Jacqueline Simpson, Roy Vickery. In Christian times, mince pies came to symbolize the birth of Jesus. The earliest pies were baked in an oblong shape to represent the manger; the crisscross topping resembled the hay rack in a stable; the spices in the pies and the gold color of the crusts stood for the gifts brought by the Three Kings.

p. 12. *Bang pots and pans*: Germany. Courtesy Harry Hunsbedt. *Bread on a broomstick*: Northern Europe. Courtesy Joseph Aregger. Bread represents fertility and plenty; a loaf stuck on a broomstick was also intended to scare away demons.

p. 13. *Yule log*: France, Serbia, Yugoslavia, Germany. The oak tree was sacred to pre-Christian Slavs. Rituals for cutting, carrying, and lighting the log varied from place to place. *Sneeze*: Sweden. *Leave a loaf*: Northern Europe. Bread is left out not only to encourage fruitfulness and health, but also to feed the dead, who are supposed to return on Christmas Eve. *Blow out a candle*: Norway, general in northern Europe. Courtesy Harry Hunsbedt. In early Christian times, bees were said to come from Paradise; so beeswax candles might have great powers of divination.

p. 14. *Animal food*: France. *If the moon shines*: Provence, France. Unlike the sun, the moon was regarded as infertile, not beneficial to crops.

p. 15. *Twelve onions*: Schleswig-Holstein, Germany. *Four more onions*: Britain.

p. 16. *Christmas bread*: Sweden. *Stars*: Russia.

p. 17. *Old-fashioned game*: Attributed to France, mid-fifteenth century. Courtesy Tatiana Davidson.

p. 18. *Open your front door*: England, Scotland. In some parts of Europe, the door of the barn was left open so bad spirits could leave through it instead of raising the roof. *Tie a rope*: Schleswig-Holstein, Germany. Courtesy Holger Janssen. *Eat an apple*: England.

p. 19. *Mix a cake*: Gloucestershire, England. Courtesy Jacqueline Simpson. This ritual is known as "baking the dumb cake."

p. 20. *Guard the pies*: England, general throughout Europe. *Shoes in a row*: Scandinavia. *Slips of paper*: Spain. This ritual is called "the urn of fate." In a variation, gifts substitute for names.

p. 21. *If your dog howls*: England.

p. 22. *"Welcome, Father Christmas!"* Scotland. Courtesy Jacqueline Simpson. This practice was called "letting in the Yule." *Broom*: Scotland. Courtesy Jacqueline Simpson.

p. 23. *Feed your pets*: United States. Courtesy Constance Bickford. *Raw egg*: England. *New leather shoes*: Hertfordshire, England. The pagan practice of wearing animal hides at new year celebrations was prohibited by the early church. The injunction against leather shoes may be a remnant of this. *Get on a swing*: Northern and southern Europe. *Ring bells*: General. *If the sun shines*: England.

p. 24. *Monday, Sunday*: England. *Tuesday, Wednesday, Thursday, Friday, Saturday*: France. *Freezing weather*: England.

p. 25. *Windy Christmas*: France. *Sunburn*: France. *Heart-shaped box*: Denmark. Courtesy Ulla Jorgensen. *Don't haul*: Denmark. Courtesy Ulla Jorgensen. The turning of wheels was thought to imply impatience with the sun. In England at one time, the church prohibited spinning on Christmas. *Don't give anything away*: England.

p. 26. *Unlucky to give away fire*: England. If fire from the Yule log was given away, the good luck associated with the Yule log would also go out of the house. *Never wash*: General. *Hug an apple tree*: Germany. *Green branch*: Ancient Rome. Long before the Christian era, evergreens were thought to have magical properties, since they stayed green all winter, and symbolized eternal life and fertility.

p. 27. *Holly and mistletoe*: England. *Two kinds of holly*: England. *Six holly leaves*: Britain. *Step on a holly berry*: England.

p. 28. *A tiny candle*: Northern Europe. *Keep holly berries*: General. *Keep the mistletoe*: Staffordshire, England. Since the evergreen symbolized fertility, destroying or discarding it could threaten the success of next year's crop.

p. 29. *Holly on the beehive*: England. *Give your cow a present*: Spain. The cow is believed to have been one of the animals that kept the infant Jesus warm through the night with their breath. Throughout Europe, cattle are given extra feed and are treated with care and respect at Christmastime.

p. 30. *Take your horse*: Bohemia. *If you wash your horse*: Northern Europe.

p. 31. *Sleepy hen*: attributed to Russia.

p. 32. *Cricket*: England. *A rat or a mouse*: Denmark. Courtesy Ulla Jorgensen. *Bad luck to go fishing*: Orkney and Shetland Islands, Britain. Journal entries from the Western Isles (ca. 1857) record men going to fish on Christmas Day and rowing 707 strokes out to sea, as they believed Christ required Peter to do. Peter found tribute money in the mouth of a fish and gave it to the poor; whatever fish was caught at Christmas in these islands would go to the poor.

p. 33. *Be sure to eat*: Denmark. Courtesy Ulla Jorgensen. *Shake the crumbs*: Germany. This magical plant was called the crumbwort. *Bury the bones*: Czechoslovakia, but probably widespread.

p. 34. *Cake brushed with dew*: Germany. *Take cake to sea*: France. Courtesy Claude Mauron.

p. 35. *When you have a cold*: France. *Mix crumbs with food*: Northern Germany. *Mix cake with seed*: Middle Europe.

p. 36. *Hit a log*: Provence, France. Courtesy Claude Mauron. A ritual to divine the fruitfulness of animals; ashes from the Yule log were said to promote fertility. *An old shoe*: Greece. Intended to scare off evil spirits called *kallikantzaroi*, ferocious half-humans, half-monsters who hid in chimneys between dawn and dusk, trying to wreck homes and consume the Christmas dinner. An alternative was to appease them by hanging offerings of bones, sausages, or candy in the chimney.

p. 37. *Tip your hat*: England. *Keep the log*: France. Saving the remains of one year's log to kindle the new one symbolizes the continuity of life, eternal fire.

p. 38. *Charcoal under your bed*: General. *Bury ashes*: General. *If you hurt yourself*: France. Courtesy Claude Mauron. Ashes from the Yule log were thought to protect houses from lightning and to bring health to the inhabitants. In Italy, the ashes were preserved as protection against hail.

p. 39. *If your family is apart*: United States. Courtesy Constance Bickford.

p. 40. *Wear something new*: Sweden. *Mud on your shoes*: Sussex, England, nineteenth century. Courtesy Jacqueline Simpson.

p. 41. *Wind from the south, east, north*: France. *Bread outside the house*: Devon, England. Courtesy Jacqueline Simpson.

p. 42. *Two wooden sticks*: Greece. Originally, wild olive branches were specified. *Eggplant*: Japan. To dream of an eggplant (signifying fruitfulness), a falcon (persistence and success), or Mount Fuji (great good fortune) is said to mean good luck at the Japanese new year.

p. 43. *"White rabbit, black hares"*: England. Courtesy Cecil R. Humphery-Smith. *White horse*: General. White horses are a universal good luck symbol.

p. 44. *A tall man*: Britain. Courtesy Jacqueline Simpson, and Ulster Folk and Transport Museum, Holywood, Northern Ireland. A custom known as "first footing." Usually a light-haired or red-haired man (possibly because of a resemblance to Norse invaders, or to Judas Iscariot) or a woman would be considered unlucky as a first footer. Professional firstfooters could be hired to enter homes, thus assuring good luck. *Sweep in good luck*: Northern Europe.

p. 45. *Grapes*: United States. Courtesy Kitty Costikyan. *Cabbage or spinach*: United States.

p. 46. *Don't give anything away*: Shropshire, England. Courtesy Jacqueline Simpson. *Never wash clothes*: Denmark. Variant, "or you will wash somebody right out of the house": Devon, England. Courtesy Jacqueline Simpson.

p. 47. *Seven is a lucky number*: Armenia.

p. 48. *Drink a toast*: General throughout Europe.

p. 49. *Cake with a bean*: General throughout Europe. The widespread tradition of choosing a mock monarch of a festival by lots is thought to go back to the Roman Saturnalia. The form described here was practiced in sixteenth-century France; the cake was called *le gateau des rois*. In some places an almond, a pea, or a coin, instead of a bean, marked the lucky slice.

p. 50. *Cake on an ox's horn*: England.

p. 51. *Visit the oldest apple tree*: England. This widespread custom was called "wassailing the apple tree"; "wassail" is from the Anglo-Saxon *waes haeil*, "good health." In Germany, guns are fired into the branches as part of the celebration.

p. 52. *Say this poem*: England. Courtesy Jacqueline Simpson.

Bibliography

Banks, M. MacLeod. *British Calendar Customs: Orkney and Shetland*. London: Wm. Glaisher, Ltd. for the Folk-Lore Society, 1946.

_____. *British Calendar Customs: Scotland*. London: Wm. Glaisher, Ltd. for the Folk-Lore Society, 1937-41.

Cagner, Ewart, Axel-Nilsson, Göran, and Sandblad, Henrik. *Swedish Christmas*. Gothenburg: Tre Tryckare, 1954.

Chassany, Jean-Philippe. *Dictionnaire de météorologie populaire*. Paris: Editions G.-P. Maisonneuve et Larose, 1970.

Debrie, René. *Contribution à l'étude des cérémonies traditionelles en Basse-Picardie*. Paris: Sinet-Grandvilliers, 1969.

Del Re, Gerard, and Del Re, Patricia. *The Christmas Almanack*. Garden City, N.Y.: Doubleday & Co., 1979.

Foley, Daniel J. *Christmas the World Over*. Radnor, Pa.: Chilton Book Co., 1963.

Frazer, Sir James G. *The Golden Bough: A Study in Magic and Religion*. 3d ed. New York: Macmillan, 1935.

Hand, Wayland D., ed. *Popular Beliefs and Superstitions from North Carolina*. The Frank C. Brown Collection of North Carolina Folklore, vols. 6 and 7. Durham, N.C.: Duke University Press, 1961, 1964.

Hole, Christina. *British Folk Customs*. London: Hutchinson Publishing Ltd., 1976.

Hottes, Alfred C. *1,001 Christmas Facts and Fancies*. New York: Dodd, Mead & Co., 1944.

Krythe, Maymie R. *All About Christmas*. New York: Harper & Brothers, 1954.

Leach, Maria, and Fried, Jerome, eds. *Funk & Wagnalls Standard Dictionary of Folklore, Mythology and Legend*. New York: Funk & Wagnalls, 1972.

Metropolitan Museum of Art Bulletin, Vol. XXXVIII, no. 2 (Fall, 1980).

Miles, Clement A. *Christmas Customs and Traditions: Their History and Significance*. (Reprint of *Christmas in Ritual and Tradition, Christian and Pagan*; 1912.) New York: Dover Publications, 1976.

Pageantry of Christmas, The. The Life Book of Christmas, vol. 2. New York: Time, Inc., 1963.

Perham, Beatrice. *Christmas: Its Origins, Music & Traditions*. Chicago: Neil A. Kjos Music Co., 1937.

Sansom, William. *A Book of Christmas*. New York: McGraw-Hill Book Co., 1968.

Barbara Heine Costikyan

has a special interest in Christmas lore because she was born on Christmas Day. After graduating from Smith College, Ms. Costikyan pursued a career in magazine publishing. A former editor of *Esquire*, she is now a contributing editor of *New York Magazine*, specializing in food columns, restaurant reviews, and personality profiles. She has three grown children and one grandchild, and lives with her husband in New York City.

Joyce Audy dos Santos

received her art training at Massachusetts College of Art and the Harvard School of Design. Her work has appeared in educational materials and in many magazines. She has taught art to children and illustrated several children's books, and is the author-illustrator of *Henri and the Loup-Garou*. She lives with her three children in Merrimac, Massachusetts.